Plainfield Public Library

Presented by
Mead Witter
Foundation, Inc.
2011 Library
Grant Program

PLAINFIELD PUBLIC LIBRARY
126 South Main Street
P.O. Box 305
Plainfield, WI 54966-0305

by Darlene R. Stille

Content Adviser:
Harold Marcuse, PhD, Associate Professor,
Department of History, University of California, Santa Barbara

Reading Adviser:
Alexa Sandmann, EdD,
Professor of Literacy, College and Graduate School
of Education, Health, and Human Services, Kent State University

COMPASS POINT BOOKS
a capstone imprint

Compass Point Books
151 Good Counsel Drive
P.O. Box 669
Mankato, MN 56002-0669

Copyright © 2011 by Compass Point Books, a Capstone imprint.
All rights reserved. No part of this book may be reproduced without written permission from the publisher. The publisher takes no responsibility for the use of any of the materials or methods described in this book, nor for the products thereof.

Editor: Brenda Haugen
Designer: Ashlee Suker
Media Researcher: Svetlana Zhurkin
Library Consultant: Kathleen Baxter
Production Specialist: Sarah Bennett
Cartographer: XNR Productions, Inc.

On the cover:
Adolf Hitler, dictator of Nazi Germany

Image Credits
Corbis/Bettmann, cover; DVIC/NARA, 7, 24, 27, 35, 39; Franklin D. Roosevelt Library, 56; Getty Images: Imagno, 11, Keystone, 17, New York Daily News Archive/John Treslian, 28; Library of Congress, 8; Newscom, 5, 13, 15, 19, 21, 23, 29, 31, 37, 40, 54, 58 (top), 59 (all); Shutterstock: posztos, 45, Steve Broer, 55; United States Holocaust Memorial Museum: Archiv der KZ-Gedenkstaette Mauthausen, courtesy of Albert Barkin Hans Marschalek, 53, courtesy of Benjamin Lefkowitz, 44, courtesy of David Mendels, 36, 58 (bottom), courtesy of Rafael Scharf, 32, National Archives and Records Administration, 34, 50, 51, National Archives and Records Administration, Federation Nationale des Deportes et Internes Resistants et Patriotes, courtesy of David Crown, 47, Yad Vashem, 41, 43.

 This book was manufactured with paper containing at least 10 percent post-consumer waste.

Library of Congress Cataloging-in-Publication Data
Stille, Darlene R.
   Architects of the Holocaust / by Darlene R. Stille.
      p. cm.—(The Holocaust)
   Includes bibliographical references and index.
   ISBN 978-0-7565-4392-1 (library binding)
   ISBN 978-0-7565-4441-6 (paperback)
   1. Holocaust, Jewish (1939–1945)—Juvenile literature. 2. Holocaust, Jewish (1939–1945)—Causes—Juvenile literature. 3. Germany—Politics and government—1933–1945—Juvenile literature. 4. Germany—Ethnic relations—History—20th century—Juvenile literature. I. Title. II. Series.
D804.34.S75 2011
   940.53'18—dc22   2010026493

Visit Compass Point Books on the Internet at *www.capstonepub.com*

Printed in the United States of America in Stevens Point, Wisconsin.
092010
005934WZS11

Table of Contents

CHAPTER 1 How Hitler Came to Power - - - - - - 5

CHAPTER 2 Lies Big Enough - - - - - - - - - - 17

CHAPTER 3 The "Need" for Living Space - - - 24

CHAPTER 4 Persecuting the Jews - - - - - - - - 29

CHAPTER 5 The Final Solution - - - - - - - - - 35

CHAPTER 6 Never Again - - - - - - - - - - - - 47

Timeline - - - - - - - - - - - - - - - - - - 58
Glossary - - - - - - - - - - - - - - - - - - 60
Additional Resources - - - - - - - - - - - 61
Select Bibliography - - - - - - - - - - - - 62
Source Notes - - - - - - - - - - - - - - - 63
Index - - - - - - - - - - - - - - - - - - - 64

Preface

In 1933 an Austrian-born politician named Adolf Hitler became the chancellor of Germany. Hitler was the leader of the National Socialist German Workers Party—the Nazi Party. Hitler was bitterly anti-Semitic and blamed the Jews for Germany's economic problems.

Hitler dreamed of populating Europe with Aryans, members of what he called a master race. The Aryans included Germans with fair skin, blond hair, and blue eyes. Hitler believed Jews were the enemy of the Aryans, and he developed a plan to isolate and kill them. Hitler called his plan the Final Solution of the Jewish Question.

With Hitler in power, life for Jewish people in Germany became increasingly difficult and dangerous. By the mid-1930s, Jewish businesses were boycotted and vandalized. Jewish Germans were forced to identify themselves by wearing the Star of David on their clothing. Jewish children were expelled from German schools. Jews were forced to leave their homes and live in certain areas, apart from Aryans, and they lost their German citizenship. Hitler's police beat and killed some Jews on the streets.

The Nazis sent millions of Jews to concentration camps in many parts of Europe. Some camps were killing centers; others were prison and forced-labor camps. Prisoners were beaten and subjected to painful experiments in which they could be maimed or killed. Survival was rare. Prisoners who were not killed in the gas chambers or shot by guards often died of starvation or illness. Besides Jews, the camps held political prisoners, homosexuals, Jehovah's Witnesses, disabled people, and people who were called gypsies.

Hitler's troops invaded Austria, Czechoslovakia, and Poland, and France and Great Britain declared war on Germany September 3, 1939. World War II became a fight between the Allies—led by France, Great Britain, the United States, and the Soviet Union—and the Axis powers of Germany, Italy, and Japan.

Until their defeat in 1945, the Nazis killed 11 million people in more than a dozen countries. Six million were Jews—two-thirds of the Jewish population in Europe. More than a million Jewish children were killed. This genocide became known as the Holocaust.

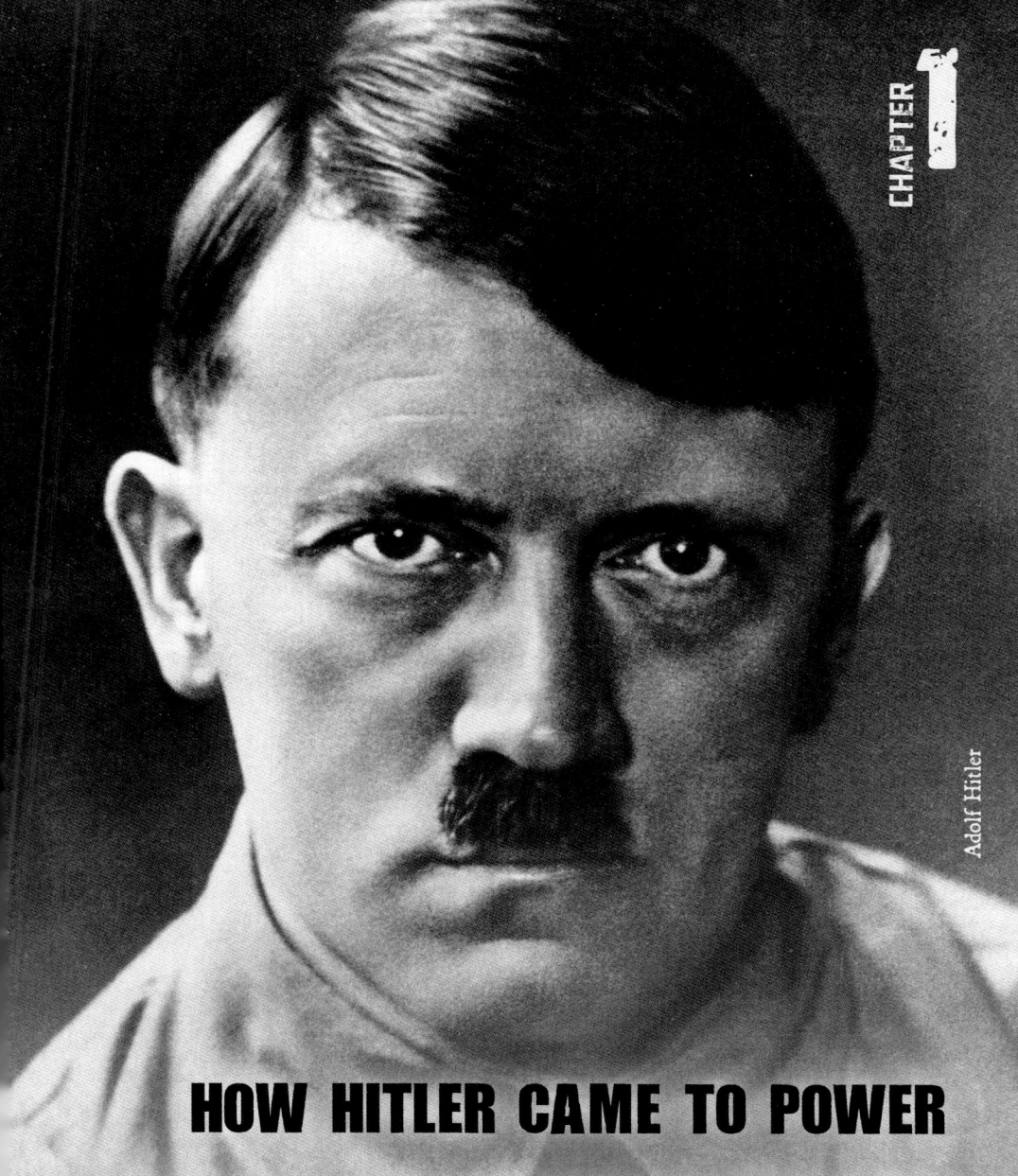

Adolf Hitler

CHAPTER 1

HOW HITLER CAME TO POWER

After seizing control of the German government in 1933, Adolf Hitler and his Nazi followers made plans to remove all Jews from Germany. However, the story of how Hitler tried to carry out these plans as Germany's dictator actually began when World War I ended.

From 1914 to 1918, Germany and the other Central Powers—Austria-Hungary, the Ottoman Empire, and Bulgaria—fought World War I against the

> The sight of all those flags, the blood red flag, you know, with the swastika, struck terror, really terror into me. ... I was very scared on the train, especially at the borders. But fortunately I got through and then, as I sat with this woman, she said, "You're an American, you can get out of here, we can't, no country wants us. ... Go out and scream! Scream so the whole world will know what we're suffering here. Just get out."
>
> —Ruth Gruber, born in Germany in 1911, recalling her return visit in 1935

Allies, which included the United Kingdom, France, and Russia. At first the Central Powers appeared to be winning the war. Then, in 1917, the United States joined the conflict on the side of the Allies. With the help of U.S. troops, the Allies won the war.

Treaty of Versailles

World War I officially ended when Germany agreed to the tough terms the Allies presented in the Treaty of Versailles. Germany lost territory in Europe, as well as its colonies in Africa. Germany was forbidden to have an air force, and the size of the German army was limited to 100,000 troops. The Allies also required Germany to pay $33 billion in war damages.

Big changes came to the government of Germany after World War I. When the war began, an emperor, called a kaiser, had governed Germany. Just before the armistice, German workers and soldiers overthrew the kaiser to allow the creation of a democracy.

An Allied gun crew fired on German soldiers during a World War I battle.

The democracy was called the Weimar Republic because the new republic's national legislature met in Weimar, Germany. The Weimar Republic had an elected parliament and an elected president. The president appointed a chancellor, who was the head of the government.

A Weak Nation

From the beginning the Weimar Republic faced many problems. There were few jobs available. Economic troubles made German money, called marks, almost worthless. The hard-working people of

Germany were shocked. How could this have happened? They did not know whom or what to blame. Many thought there must be some kind of conspiracy behind the country's misfortune.

Political groups on both the far left and the far right wanted to take advantage of the situation and overthrow the democratic government. On the far left were Communists. Under a Communist system, the government would own all mines, factories, and other places of industry.

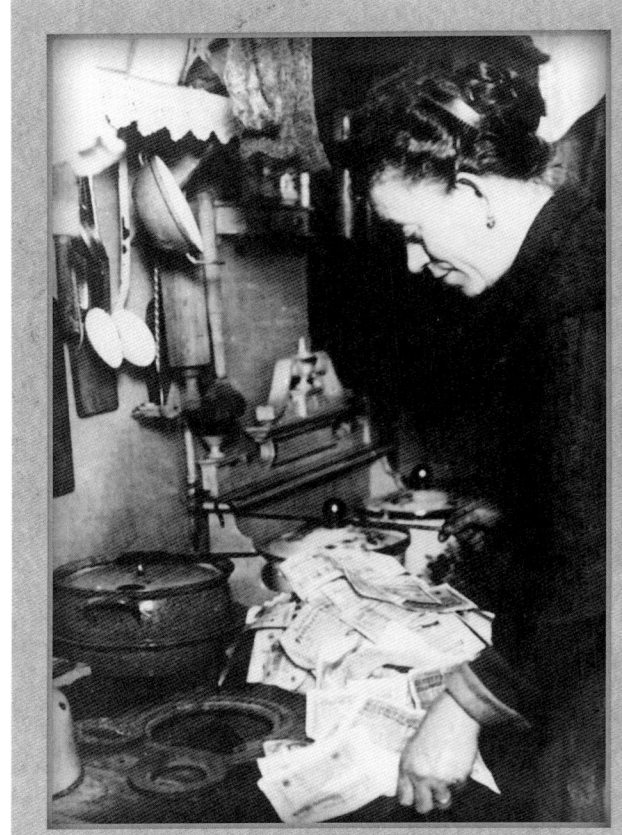

A woman in Berlin, Germany's capital, used her nearly worthless German money to fuel her stove.

On the right were army officers and other conservative German leaders who resented the republic. They remained loyal to the kaiser and the empire. They believed that the empire had provided a better system of government.

To the right of the conservatives were the Fascists. They believed in a strong, authoritarian, nationalistic government.

Nationalists tend to believe that their country is superior to all other countries. Many also believe that one ethnic group is superior to all others. In Italy Fascists headed by Benito Mussolini gained power in 1922. Three years later Mussolini became the fascist dictator of Italy.

The Fascists in Germany included the Nazis. Under their leader, Adolf Hitler, the Nazis tried to overthrow the Weimar Republic in 1923. But by then life for the German people had improved somewhat, and the Nazi rebellion failed. Hitler was sentenced to prison.

Mein Kampf

While in prison for trying to take over the government, Hitler wrote *Mein Kampf* (*My Struggle*). The book outlined his plans to take control of Germany, wage a war to gain control of Europe, and reduce Jews to noncitizen status. When he got out of prison after serving only a year of his sentence, the Nazi Party was unknown to most Germans. However, within a few years, the country was again in chaos. Although things had been improving, the worldwide Great Depression began in 1929. In the early 1930s millions of Germans lost their jobs.

Hitler saw this situation as a great opportunity. He had not been able to gain control of Germany through violent means. Now he

Hitler Discovers His Talent

Adolf Hitler became a social misfit after he failed to achieve his dream of becoming an artist. He was rejected twice by the Academy of Fine Arts in Vienna, Austria. Hitler lived a lonely life and supported himself by painting postcards and ads. After World War I began, he volunteered for the German army. He eventually became a corporal and won medals for bravery. He loved the comradeship of the military and what he saw as the glory of war. After the war Hitler joined the newly formed German Workers Party and directed its propaganda. He was good at the job. He also discovered a talent for making speeches and raising money. In 1921, with help from admiring friends, he became leader of the party, which was then being called the Nazi Party.

was determined to try to gain control by legal means. The German people were looking for new leadership. They increasingly supported political parties that promised a new system of government.

Hitler led the Nazis into the streets to protest what they called the inefficiency and corruption of the Weimar Republic. They also protested against the unfairness of the Treaty of Versailles. The Nazis claimed to be the only party that represented all German people—all Germans who were not Jewish, that is. Nazi candidates ran for office, and Nazi campaigns took a violent turn. A private army called the Sturmabteilung (SA) protected Hitler's political rallies. They also beat and threatened communists and other opponents and broke up their political rallies. More and more people heard Hitler's message—and they liked what he said.

Nazi Promises

Hitler and the Nazis promised to bring stability to Germany. They vowed to put people back to work and to restore traditional German values and national pride. Hitler was a powerful public speaker. Waving his arms and raising his voice, he promised to ignore the Treaty of Versailles and re-establish Germany's military power.

A truck loaded with an anti-Semitic poster and a Nazi flag spread hatred of Jews in Vienna, Austria, and urged people to support Nazi candidates for office.

He blamed the Jews and communists for Germany's defeat in World War I and for the nation's troubles.

The Nazis' promises appealed to great numbers of Germans, and the popularity of the Nazi movement soared. Wealthy industrialists donated money to help elect Nazis because Hitler promised to help them. Conservatives, including many wealthy people, supported the Nazis because they saw an opportunity to regain privileges and status they had lost when the German empire fell during World War I. Army officers were attracted by Hitler's promise to break the terms of the Treaty of Versailles and rebuild the German military. Growing numbers of people decided to vote for Nazi candidates. In the 1932 parliamentary elections, Hitler's Nazis won about one-third of the votes. Hitler demanded to be made chancellor of Germany.

Chancellor Hitler

The Weimar Republic was largely held together by its president, Paul von Hindenburg, and the chancellor, whom he chose. Von Hindenburg was one of the most beloved people in Germany. He had been Germany's supreme military commander during World War I and had won battles at the beginning of the war. Despite Germany's ultimate loss, people saw him as a war hero. Germans elected him president in 1925 and re-elected him in 1932. But von Hindenburg was growing old and feeble.

At first von Hindenburg refused to appoint Hitler as chancellor. He didn't like or trust Hitler. Industrialists and conservative politicians, however, convinced von Hindenburg that he should make Hitler chancellor just to bring some stability to the government. The conservatives believed that they could control Hitler and use him to regain political power for themselves. Von Hindenburg finally gave in. He assumed that Hitler would keep his promise to abide by German laws. He appointed Hitler the chancellor of Germany January 30, 1933.

President Paul von Hindenburg (left) was failing mentally and physically when he appointed Adolf Hitler chancellor of Germany in January 1933.

But von Hindenburg and many others had greatly underestimated Hitler. As soon as he became chancellor of Germany, he started to destroy its democratic system of government. The month after Hitler became chancellor, a suspicious fire burned the Reichstag, Germany's parliament building. Hitler blamed the communists for the blaze and was granted emergency powers.

He also demanded new elections in March, and the Nazis won 44 percent of the vote. Even though this was not a majority, Germany's lawmakers passed the Enabling Act. This act allowed the executive branch of government to create laws without the consent of the legislative branch. In effect, it allowed Hitler to set up a dictatorship.

Hitler outlawed all political parties except the Nazi Party. The Nazis seized control of all parts of the German government, from the courts and police to schools. They also took control of newspapers. Soon the Nazis controlled every aspect of German life. Any German who dared to speak out against the Nazis was beaten, killed, deported, or sent off to the concentration camps that the Nazis were beginning to set up around Germany. The first permanent concentration camp, called Dachau, opened near Munich in 1933. Its first inmates were Germans who opposed Hitler.

Few Germans, however, openly opposed Hitler. Some Germans

agreed with everything the Nazis did. Others remained silent because they agreed with most of the Nazis' policies. Some Germans were upset by the Nazis' tactics, but they remained silent because they feared being imprisoned or murdered by Hitler's SA.

Political prisoners were forced to work in German concentration camps in the 1930s.

The Fuhrer

When von Hindenburg died in 1934, Hitler declared himself the Fuhrer—Germany's leader. Many Germans supported this move. Enthusiastic crowds greeted Hitler wherever he went. They extended their right arms in a Nazi salute, shouting "Heil Hitler!" (Hail Hitler!) or "Sieg Heil!" (Hail victory!). A military organization of elite troops called the Schutzstaffel (SS) was created as Hitler's security force. The SS eventually evolved into the Nazi Party's most ruthless private police force. It grew to more than 1 million troops and carried out many of the Nazis' war crimes.

Hitler declared that he would build an empire—the Third Reich—that would last 1,000 years. He did build an empire, but it lasted little more than 10 years. During that time Hitler and the Nazis murdered millions of innocent people and brought about the almost total destruction of Germany.

CHAPTER 2

Joseph Goebbels

> If you tell a lie big enough and keep repeating it, people will eventually come to believe it.
>
> —Joseph Goebbels, Nazi minister of propaganda

LIES BIG ENOUGH

From the beginning of his quest for power in the 1920s, Adolf Hitler planned to dominate all of Europe and remove every Jew from Germany by any means possible. He knew he would need the enthusiastic support of the German people.

Jews had lived in Germany for centuries. Jewish Germans lived peacefully next to their non-Jewish neighbors. Jews and non-Jews attended school together, served together in the army during World War I, and worked side by side in all kinds of businesses. Jews were respected doctors, scientists, artists, and musicians. They operated tailor shops, grocery stores, and many other kinds of businesses all over Germany. Many Jews and non-Jews were friends. To stir up intense hatred of Jews, Hitler knew, he would have to present a powerful argument showing that Jews were evil and intended to harm Germany. His message would have to persuade non-Jewish Germans to shun their former friends and co-workers.

Persuading the Masses

The Nazis created propaganda that appealed to Germans disheartened by the loss of World War I and the economic troubles of the late 1920s and early 1930s. Propaganda is biased or often misleading information used to promote a particular cause. The Nazis became masters of propaganda and its use to control the masses. Hitler believed that by telling a big enough lie often enough, the Nazis could make people believe it.

Nazi propaganda began with the false notion that non-Jewish Germans belonged to a superior Aryan race of white western European people. The propaganda told the German people that being a racially pure Aryan was more important than a person's religion, social class, or birthplace. The propaganda was used in an attempt to convince the citizens that racially pure Germans had a duty to work together for the good of all Aryans in the Fatherland, a name the Nazis gave to Germany. In Nazi propaganda, it was the nation, not the individual, that was important.

In *Mein Kampf* Hitler wrote that propaganda should be used to spread the Nazi doctrine of anti-Semitism and anti-Communism among the German people. In speeches, on posters, and in Nazi Party pamphlets and other publications, the Nazis often portrayed members of opposing political parties as Communists. They labeled as Communists even the Social Democratic Party, a large, moderate political party. Nazi propaganda also

The cover of a 1937 anti-Semitic Nazi propaganda book showed a Jew holding gold coins in one hand and a piece of communist territory in his left arm. It was meant to depict Jews as ugly, greedy, and corrupt.

tried to link Jews with Communists and claimed that Jews were behind the Communist revolution in Russia.

Goebbels' Ministry of Propaganda

After becoming chancellor, Hitler chose a master of propaganda to carry the Nazi message. He named Joseph Goebbels to head the new National Ministry of Public Enlightenment and Propaganda. Goebbels had been in charge of Nazi propaganda since 1928 and had helped Hitler rise to power. Like Hitler he understood that if Nazi plans for world domination were to succeed, the German people would have to believe that they were members of an elite group. Jews, Communists, and people with physical and mental disabilities were outsiders. The Nazis blamed Jews and Communists, along with the Allied nations, as being responsible for unemployment, inflation, and nearly all other problems in Germany.

Goebbels made sure that Nazi propaganda about racial superiority was not just carried to the German people by speeches or in Nazi Party publications. He extended the message of racial purity and hatred of Jews to German theater productions, movies, radio programs, educational materials, newspapers, and magazines. Films, for example, portrayed Jews as inferior creatures determined to do evil. They portrayed Aryans as wholesome heroes.

German Youth

The Nazis realized how important young people were to their success. In 1933 they set up an organization called Hitler Youth, for German boys ages 13 to 18. The League of German Girls was designed for girls 14 to 18. In 1936 the Nazis required all German boys to belong to Hitler Youth. When World War II began, about 8 million boys were in the group.

The Nazis taught the young people their message of racial superiority and hatred for Jews. They also encouraged children to

Hitler Youth drummers took part in Nazi rallies in the 1930s.

> **Schoolchildren and the Nazis**
>
> Fifteen-year-old Emma Mogilensky felt the great change that had come to Germany when she arrived at school with other Jewish students one morning. "... All the other children had formed two lines in front of the school house door and as we walked through those two lines they beat us up!" she said. "I went to the teacher and I complained and he said, 'Well, what did you expect, you dirty Jew?'" Emma and her Jewish friends then realized that the teacher had told the other students to beat the Jewish children as they entered the school.

spy on their parents and teachers and to report anyone who criticized the Nazis. The Nazis purged the schools of Jewish teachers and non-Jewish teachers who did not agree with Nazi aims.

Parades and Rallies

To give the German people a sense of belonging to a great mass movement, the Nazis staged dramatic parades and huge rallies in Berlin, the capital, and other cities. Soldiers and members of Nazi organizations carried hundreds of red flags with swastikas through the streets.

The grandest rallies took place in Nuremberg, a city where the Nazis held their party conventions almost every year during the 1920s and 1930s. After the Nazis seized power in 1933, as many as 500,000

From a car on the field, Adolf Hitler saluted spectators who were attending a Nazi rally in Nuremberg, Germany.

soldiers, Hitler Youth, Nazi officials, and members of other groups assembled for the rallies. They marched in parades, watched Nazi films, and listened to speeches by Hitler and other Nazi leaders. New laws taking away rights from Jews were announced at these rallies.

The Nazi propaganda worked. Ordinary German people accepted the Nazi message about the superiority of Aryans. Ordinary non-Jewish Germans were ready to watch their Jewish friends and neighbors be persecuted and sent away. Ordinary Germans believed it was the duty of Germany to take back land in surrounding countries that was rightfully theirs. They were ready to invade surrounding lands and march into what became World War II.

A Sudeten woman couldn't hide her misery as she dutifully saluted the triumphant Hitler.

CHAPTER 3

> I have put my death-head formations in place with the command ... to send into death many women and children of Polish origin and language. Only thus we can gain the living space that we need.
>
> —Adolf Hitler

THE "NEED" FOR LIVING SPACE

The horrors of the Holocaust were unseen by the rest of the world because Germany was at war. World War II broke out after Hitler began to invade other European nations. He began the invasion after he had convinced the German people that they were entitled to the land.

According to the Nazis, the growing German population needed *Lebensraum* (living space). They said Germany had to increase the amount of land it controlled in Europe. Therefore German policies toward other nations were based in part on the need for more land. The Nazis also played on German resentment over the loss of land after World War I. The Treaty of Versailles gave pieces of land where many people of German descent lived to Belgium, France, Czechoslovakia, Poland, and Denmark.

Besides preparing Germany for the coming conflict over land, Hitler began testing the will of other nations to oppose him. First he violated the Treaty of Versailles by building up the German army. In 1938 Germany invaded Austria and made it part of Germany. Hitler correctly guessed that no other nation would try to stop him.

Later the same year, he demanded that Germany be given a part of Czechoslovakia called the Sudetenland. The Sudetenland had been part of Austria-Hungary before World War I. About 3 million Germans lived there. In an attempt to keep peace, France and Great Britain forced Czechoslovakia to give the Sudetenland to Germany in 1938. Hitler then grew even bolder and invaded Czechoslovakia in 1939.

Despite Hitler's hatred of Communism, Germany and the

Turned Away

Liane Reif lived with her parents in a 14-room apartment in Vienna, Austria, until the Nazis took over. Her father, a dentist, was found dead one day. The family believed he had committed suicide. Liane's mother, with more than 900 other Jewish refugees, booked passage in 1939 aboard the *St. Louis*, a ship bound for Cuba. But Cuba turned the refugees away, and so did the United States. Eventually Great Britain, France, Belgium, and the Netherlands took in the 937 refugees. But the Nazis soon conquered all these countries except Great Britain. After the Nazi takeover, many of those who had been aboard the *St. Louis* were sent with other Jews to concentration camps, where many of them died. Liane survived. She and her family had been in France, but when Germany invaded the country, the Reifs were able to take a train and escape to the unoccupied French city of Limoges, where many Jews fled. Liane recalled, "At first we were housed in a stadium used for circus performances. ... We had hardly any food. ... On my sixth birthday my mother brought me the nicest present I'd ever had—a peach and some dried fruit."

Soviet Union secretly agreed to attack Poland and divide it between them. On September 1, 1939, Germany invaded Poland.

World War II Begins

The invasion of Poland did not go unchallenged. Great Britain and France had promised to defend Poland from German attack. So they declared war on Nazi Germany. German forces quickly conquered Denmark, Norway, the Netherlands, Belgium, Luxembourg, and France. Meanwhile the Soviet Union also invaded Poland, then Finland and several countries in eastern Europe. Hitler, who had always wanted the riches of the Soviet Union and hated Communism, broke his secret agreement and invaded the Soviet Union in June 1941. In the west the British fought Germany alone until December 1941. By then Germany had defense agreements with two other dictatorships—Italy and Japan. Together the three countries were called the Axis.

On December 7, 1941, Japanese planes bombed the United States naval fleet in Pearl Harbor, Hawaii. After the attack the United States declared war on the Axis powers and joined World War II, which was already well under way.

The USS *Shaw* exploded during the Japanese bombing of Pearl Harbor in 1941.

Scientist Albert Einstein, his daughter Margot (right), and his secretary Helen Dukes were sworn in as U.S. citizens in 1940. They had fled Germany.

A Problem with Conquest

While Germany was invading other countries, the Gestapo secret police agents were trying to rid Germany of its Jewish citizens. As the Nazis had hoped, many Jews fled Germany. But as German troops conquered country after country, Jews in the conquered lands fell under the rule of Nazi Germany. Instead of ridding the Third Reich of Jews, the Nazis were increasing the number of Jews under German rule.

The measures that the Nazis took against the Jews of Europe became increasingly brutal. Few people foresaw at the beginning of Nazi rule that Hitler's campaign against Jews would end in unimaginable slaughter.

Anti-Jewish boycott

> Our many Jewish friends and acquaintances are being taken away in droves. The Gestapo is treating them very roughly and transporting them in cattle cars.
>
> —Anne Frank, a Jewish teenager who hid from the Nazis with her family in Amsterdam

CHAPTER 4
PERSECUTING THE JEWS

After seizing control of Germany, the Nazis used the powers of government in a growing campaign of persecution against the Jews. First Nazi officials made it illegal to sell Jewish newspapers on the streets. At a September 1935 Nazi Party congress in Nuremberg, Adolf Hitler announced laws taking German citizenship away from Jews and forbidding marriage between Jewish and non-Jewish Germans. The Nazis said non-Jewish

Germans should boycott Jewish goods and businesses.

As laws taking more rights away from Jews were being passed, there was constant violence against Jewish Germans. Gangs of thugs beat and sometimes killed innocent Jews while the police stood by and allowed the violence to happen. The Nazi-controlled local governments often blamed the Jews for causing the violence.

The Night of Broken Glass

After dark on November 9, 1938, the Nazis began a massive assault on synagogues, Jewish businesses, and Jewish homes. Mobs of Nazis in cities across Germany and Austria roamed through the streets, smashing windows, setting fire to synagogues, and terrorizing the Jewish population. The violence began after a teenage Jewish Pole who had grown up in Germany shot a Nazi diplomat in Paris, France. The violence came to be called Kristallnacht, meaning the night of broken glass.

The attackers damaged about 7,500 businesses and burned 267 synagogues. Hundreds of Jews were killed. Police officers and firefighters simply stood by.

The Nazis again blamed the Jews for the destruction and fined them $400 million. They also passed a law requiring that all Jewish businesses be given to Aryans. The SS and Gestapo

Germans passed by the smashed windows of a Jewish-owned shop vandalized during Kristallnacht.

arrested about 30,000 Jewish men and boys and sent most of them to concentration camps.

Ghettos

After Germany invaded Poland, millions of Jewish Poles came under Nazi rule. The Nazis set about separating Jewish Poles from non-Jewish Poles by establishing ghettos. The ghettos were areas of cities where Jews were forced to live.

The Nazis made Jewish families leave their homes and live in horribly overcrowded conditions. The largest Polish ghetto was in Warsaw. In the Warsaw ghetto about 400,000 Jews were forced to

Jews gathered around a couple selling firewood on the street in the Warsaw ghetto.

live in a 1.3-square-mile (3.4-square-kilometer) area, which is about the same size as Central Park in New York City. Conditions were so crowded that six or seven people lived in each room. The Nazis also forced Jews to wear identifying badges or armbands and to work without pay.

Concentration Camps

The Nazis set up thousands of concentration camps where hundreds of thousands of people were held. By the end of the war, they had

Life in the Ghetto

Paula Garfinkel lived with her parents and three siblings in Lodz, Poland, where her father owned a furniture store. The family was part of the city's large Jewish population. "In early 1940," she recalled, "our family was forcibly relocated to the Lodz ghetto, where we were assigned one room for all six of us. Food was the main problem. At the women's clothing factory where I worked, I at least got some soup for lunch. But we desperately needed to find more food for my younger brother, who was very sick and bleeding internally. From the window at my factory I looked out at a potato field. Knowing that if I was caught, I'd be shot, I crept out one night to the field, dug up as many potatoes as I could, and ran home."

built more than a dozen major concentration camps, with about 20,000 branch camps, in Germany and countries that the German army had conquered. Many of the concentration camps were slave labor camps. The prisoners worked in mines, factories, road building, or construction until they died of starvation, exhaustion, disease, or mistreatment.

Nazi doctors conducted horrible medical experiments on people in concentration camps. In some experiments to benefit Nazi sailors and airmen, the doctors tested how long a person can survive in icy water or at high altitudes without oxygen. They also infected people with deadly germs that caused diseases such as tuberculosis

A guide showed containers storing human organs removed from prisoners in Buchenwald to an American soldier after the camp was liberated.

and malaria. In addition, they performed surgical operations without anesthesia. They used prisoners as human guinea pigs.

Eventually some concentration camps were used for another purpose. They were turned into death factories where the Nazis tried to kill as many people as possible.

Thousands of gold rings taken from victims at Buchenwald

> We had the moral right, we had the duty to our people to do it, to kill this people who wanted to kill us.
>
> —Heinrich Himmler, head of the SS and Gestapo

THE FINAL SOLUTION

The Nazis chose genocide as the answer to the "Jewish question" in the summer or fall of 1941. They referred to their plans for killing all the Jews in Europe as the Final Solution of the Jewish Question. After German troops invaded the Soviet Union in 1941, the mass killing of Jews soon began. The SS Death's Head Divisions were among those responsible for carrying out the killings. The men in this group wore a skull-and-bones emblem on their uniforms. Heinrich Himmler, who headed the SS and the Gestapo,

Heinrich Himmler (left) talked with SS officers while visiting the Mauthausen camp.

and Himmler's second in command, Reinhard Heydrich, were the architects of the genocide. Adolf Eichmann, a lieutenant colonel in the SS, was responsible for having Jews transported to ghettos, camps, and murder factories.

Mobile Killing Squads

As German troops advanced into Soviet territory, they were followed by special task forces whose job was to eliminate Jews. Heydrich and Eichmann directed the killing units to round up all the Jewish people living in a captured community and shoot them. At his war crimes trial after World War II, Otto Ohlendorf,

Jews were executed by German army mobile killing units near Ivangorod, Ukraine, in 1942. A resistance fighter intercepted the photo at a post office.

one of the unit leaders, explained how the mass murders were carried out.

All of the Jews were told they must register for resettlement. "After the registration the Jews were collected at one place; and from there they were later transported to the place of execution, which was, as a rule, an antitank ditch or a natural excavation," Ohlendorf testified. "The executions were carried out in a military manner, by firing squads under command. They were transported to the place of execution in trucks, always only as many as could be executed

> **Babi Yar**
>
> Babi Yar was the name of a deep ravine outside Kiev, in what was then the Soviet Republic of Ukraine. It was the site of a major massacre by Nazi mobile killing units, the SS, German police, and others.
>
> Before German troops invaded Kiev in September 1941, about 100,000 Jewish residents fled the city. About 60,000 remained behind. As revenge for explosions that destroyed German military headquarters and other buildings in Kiev, the Nazis decided to kill all of Kiev's remaining Jewish residents. The SS and police took the remaining Jews—mostly women, children, and elderly men—as well as gypsies, Communists, and Soviet prisoners of war to Babi Yar. The Nazis shot them as they lined up at the edge of the ravine. In two days the Nazis murdered almost 34,000 people there. The Nazis continued to use Babi Yar as a killing site, eventually leaving about 100,000 bodies there. Afterward they blew up the sides of the ravine to hide the corpses.

immediately. In this way it was attempted to keep the span of time from the moment in which the victims knew what was about to happen to them until the time of their actual execution as short as possible."

Shooting so many helpless victims became difficult even for the hardened SS soldiers and experienced policemen. So the Nazis invented a less personal killing device, the gas van. The SS men herded Jewish victims into a gas chamber on a truck. Then they diverted exhaust gas from the truck into the mobile gas chamber. Between 1941 and 1943 the mobile killing units murdered hundreds of thousands of Soviet Jews, disabled people, and political opponents.

Nevertheless the Nazi high command found the mobile killing units to be inefficient. They came up with another plan, death camps.

The Extermination Camps

Unlike concentration camps, where prisoners were usually used for slave labor, extermination camps were murder factories. Nazis set up extermination camps in German-occupied Poland. Each camp had one or more gas chambers, where many of the executions took place, and furnaces, called crematoriums, where the bodies were burned.

The bones of anti-Nazi German women were still in crematoriums in Buchenwald near Weimar, Germany, when the camp was liberated by American soldiers in April 1945.

The journey to a death camp began when SS soldiers or German policemen rounded up Jews from the ghettos. The SS loaded Jews into train boxcars. There were no beds or other comforts in the boxcars and little or no food. Guards shut the doors of the boxcars, and the trains set out for the death camps. Sometimes people were locked in a boxcar for days. Some people died on the way to the camps.

Adolf Eichmann managed the mass deportation of Jews to ghettos and death camps in Nazi-occupied eastern Europe.

One of the most infamous death camps was Auschwitz, in German-occupied Poland. Auschwitz was made up of three main camps. Auschwitz I opened in 1940 to hold German prisoners and Polish political prisoners. Auschwitz II, also called Birkenau, was built in 1942 as a slave labor camp, but it soon became a murder factory as well. Auschwitz III, which also opened in 1942, was a chemical factory run by slaves. Prisoners in Auschwitz III made rubber and other products for the German war effort.

Arrival at Auschwitz

Between March 1942 and November 1944, trains arrived at Auschwitz almost every day. Guards opened the boxcars, ordered the victims out, and made them line up. SS doctors inspected the lines of prisoners and determined their fates. The doctors sent most women and children, and men who looked old or sick, to the left—to the gas

Jewish prisoners were taken off a train and assembled at Auschwitz-Birkenau.

chambers. They sent some women and all men who looked healthy to the right—to be worked to death as slave laborers. An SS doctor chose a third, smaller group to be used in Nazi medical experiments. Most of these people were either twins or dwarfs.

In an interview Leo Schneiderman of Lodz, Poland, described arriving at Auschwitz. "It was late at night … the minute the gates opened up, we heard screams, barking of dogs," he said. "And then we got out of the train. And everything went so fast: left, right, right, left. Men separated from women. Children torn from the arms of mothers. The elderly chased like cattle. The sick, the disabled were handled like packs of garbage. … My mother ran over to me and grabbed me by the shoulders, and she told me, 'Liebele, I'm not going to see you no more. Take care of your brother.'"

The heads of prisoners selected to be slave laborers were shaved. Then camp workers registered the laborers and tattooed identifying numbers on their arms. Finally the prisoners received striped uniforms. By the end of the war about 405,000 slave laborers had been registered and tattooed at Auschwitz.

The Gas Chambers

Most of the people arriving at Auschwitz were not registered, however. Soon after arriving they were taken to the gas chambers

A group of Jewish women and children selected for death at Auschwitz-Birkenau waited to be taken to the gas chamber. Often there was no wait.

and killed. The operations at all the killing centers were top secret. The Nazi government didn't want the world to know about the activities in the death camps. Not even the victims knew what fate awaited them until the end. At Auschwitz the SS guards made them believe that they were being taken for a shower. The victims had to take off all of their clothes and jewelry. Then they were herded into an underground room with what looked like pipes for shower water coming from the ceiling.

As in other camps, the gas chamber at Mauthausen was designed to look like a shower room.

Some slave laborers had to help the SS with their gruesome task. Some prisoners worked as barbers, cutting off the victims' hair. The SS forced others to burn the bodies or clean up the gas chambers to get them ready for the next group. Sam Itzkowitz, a prisoner from Makow, Poland, had the task of building gas chamber doors. "[It] was a thick door, was about six inches thick," he said later. "I built it myself and I know what it's like: three bolts, three iron bars were across. The bars were laid over and then screwed tight.

"The gas chamber was also a hall ... with two ... chimneys going all the way to the ... roof. ... That's where the SS men were standing. ... When they filled in the bunker with all the women, they put the men in. ... And when the bunker was already so filled they couldn't

Cans that once contained cyanide-soaked pellets that were used to kill prisoners in the gas chambers at Auschwitz

put no more people ... they made the kids crawl on the top of the heads. ... When the door was slammed behind them ... [an SS man] put a mask on, tore the lid off of the gas ... canister, threw it down the chute ... into the gas chamber. ... And as soon as he threw the gas in, he slammed the lid shut, so the gas wouldn't escape. And all you could hear is one loud sound, 'Shema' [the Jewish declaration of faith] ... and that was all. ... In the door they had a little peephole. ... And when they turned on the light ... in the bunker, you could see whether the people were already dead or not."

More than 2 million Jews, Poles, people who were called gypsies, and Soviet prisoners of war went to their deaths in Auschwitz. The SS cremated their bodies in crematoriums, leaving nothing but ashes and bits of bone. At some camps the SS buried the bodies in mass graves or burned them in open pits.

CHAPTER 6

Concentration camp survivors

> ... I swore never to be silent whenever [and] wherever human beings endure suffering and humiliation.
>
> —Elie Wiesel, Holocaust survivor, author, and Nobel Peace Prize winner

NEVER AGAIN

The Holocaust came to an end with the defeat of Germany by Allied forces. Deep snow, brutal cold, and fierce fighting by Soviet soldiers stopped the German advance into the Soviet Union in February 1943. In June 1944 Allied troops landed in Normandy on the coast of France and began a drive to Berlin. Soviet troops went on the offensive, pushing German forces out of eastern Europe. As the Allied troops advanced from the east and the west, the Nazis

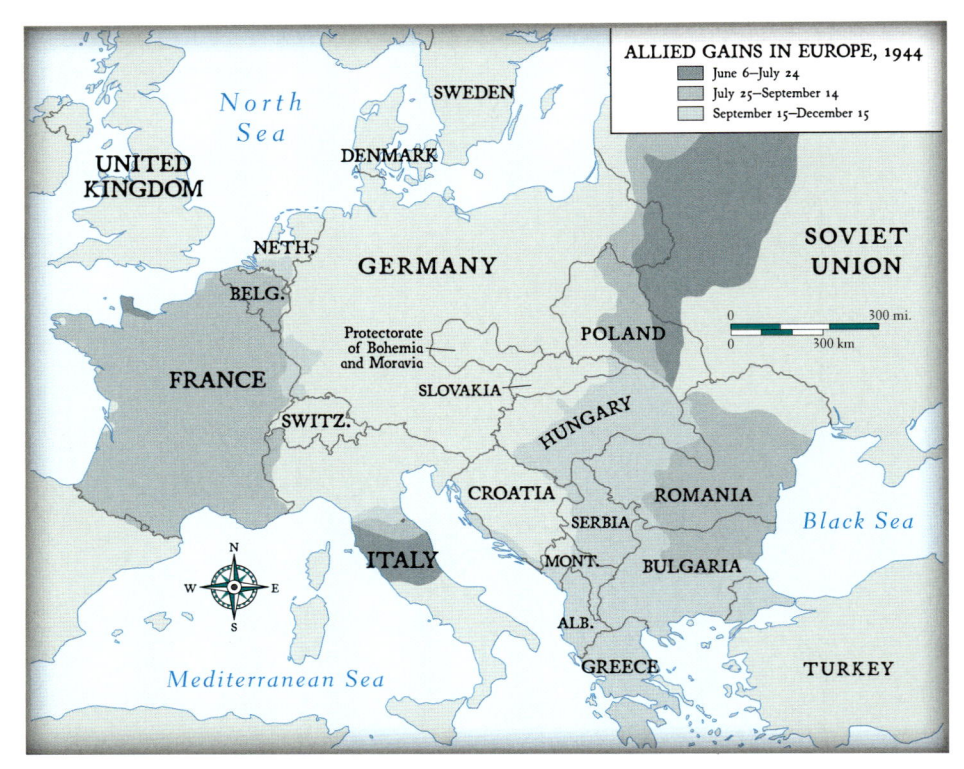

ALLIED GAINS IN EUROPE, 1944
- June 6–July 24
- July 25–September 14
- September 15–December 15

In the summer of 1944, Allied forces began advancing on Germany from both the east and the west.

stepped up their murder operations. They were determined to murder as many people as possible before Allied troops found the extermination camps. During the summer of 1944, the four gas chamber-crematorium operations at Auschwitz-Birkenau reached their maximum capacity, murdering as many as 9,000 people a day.

As the Allies came closer, the Nazis at murdering centers in Poland started taking apart gas chambers and crematoriums to try to destroy evidence of their crimes. The Allies advanced so rapidly, however, that the Nazis didn't have time to remove all the evidence.

Before Allied troops reached a camp, the SS would force the prisoners to leave. They had to march through snow and cold to other concentration camps, such as Buchenwald, in Germany. On these marches during the winter of 1944–1945, thousands of prisoners died. Many were shot when they could not go on.

Dreadful Discovery

In the spring of 1945, Allied troops entered Germany and saw the full horror of the concentration camps. They saw bodies everywhere inside the barbed wire fences. Some of the prisoners had been shot by fleeing Nazis. Others had been locked in buildings and burned alive. Some had died of malnutrition or disease.

James A. Rose, a U.S. soldier from Toledo, Ohio, recalled his impressions when he first saw the Dachau concentration camp: "Part of our division ... had troops in the camp liberating the camp. ... They opened the compound and I seen thousands of people crowding out that looked like skeletons with skin stretched on them. They were dirty, they smelled, and just one look at them, some of them half dead ... we realized [what] this war was all about, we know now why we were participating in this war."

The camp survivors found it hard to believe that they were really free. Their liberators soon realized that most survivors were

Journalists, accompanied by American military police, toured the newly liberated Buchenwald concentration camp.

very sick. Some of them, even though they had been freed, were so weakened that they died in a few days. Typhus epidemics raged through the camps. Thousands of prisoners continued to die of typhus, which is caused by a germ carried by body lice, and many were infected and sick.

Caring for the Survivors

Treating people in such poor physical condition was a great challenge. Thousands of nurses from the United States served in evacuation hospitals set up to treat the survivors. First they had to move the inmates from the filthy camp barracks. "They were so thin," said U.S. nurse Pat Lynch. "I couldn't pick any of them up. If I were to pick them up I'd tear the skin." At least three people were needed to move each survivor—one holding the person's head, one the legs, and one lifting the torso.

Once the survivors were in clean beds with clean bedding, either in tents or hospital buildings, treatment could begin. It was difficult to inject them with fluids because they had no fat and little

At an American military field hospital in Volary, Czechoslovakia, Major Frank Ankner took the pulse of a female Jewish survivor of a death march.

muscle. They really were just skin and bones. They could not eat, so nurses fed them with medicine droppers.

Many of the people died, but most gained strength and got well, little by little. They then began the job of rebuilding their lives. Some moved to the United States. Some moved to Palestine and helped to establish the state of Israel. Most of the rest moved to other countries.

Nuremberg Trials

The Allied powers decided that Nazi officials should be tried as war criminals. Some Nazis didn't wait for the Allies to judge or sentence them. Shortly before Germany surrendered, Hitler and Himmler committed suicide. The director of propaganda, Goebbels, and his wife killed their six children by poisoning them. Then Goebbels likely shot his wife and then himself.

Twenty-four top-ranking leaders of Nazi Germany were charged with war crimes. One committed suicide and another was found to be medically unfit for trial. The remaining 22 were tried by an international military tribunal in Nuremberg. Judges sentenced 12 of the defendants to death by hanging and seven to prison terms. They found three others not guilty.

Many minor Nazi officials, such as police officers, concentration camp guards, doctors, and members of killing squads, were tried by Allied military courts or in the countries where they had committed war crimes. Some of them were sentenced to death or to long prison terms. Many others were able to escape justice for decades, some forever.

The Banality of Evil

Historians and philosophers have tried to understand the complex reasons Germany allowed such horrible events to take place. One

A former prisoner at Mauthausen testified at the trial of 61 former camp staff members.

of the most famous and controversial of these experts was German-American political scientist Hannah Arendt. She attended the trial of Adolf Eichmann, who had been in charge of deporting Jews to concentration camps. He had escaped to Argentina. Israeli agents captured Eichmann, and in 1961 he was tried in Jerusalem.

Arendt wrote a book about the trial, *Eichmann in Jerusalem: A Report on the Banality of Evil*. Arendt saw the crimes of the Nazi regime as stemming from a situation in which people like Eichmann dutifully did their jobs without giving much thought to what they were doing. Rather than seeing Eichmann as a depraved criminal, she saw him as a man who put his career ahead of everything and could not think critically about what he was doing.

An Israeli guard closely watched Adolf Eichmann, who was on trial for the mass murder of Jews during World War II.

"Having encountered such a man," wrote Jerome Kohn, director of the Hannah Arendt Center in New York City, "Arendt saw that the banality of evil is potentially far greater in extent—indeed limitless—than the growth of evil from a 'root.' A root can be uprooted ... but the evil perpetrated by an Eichmann can spread over the face of the earth like a 'fungus' precisely because it has no root."

The United Nations headquarters now is in New York City.

Universal Declaration of Human Rights

As World War II came to an end, 50 nations created the United Nations. Gradually more nations joined. The U.N.'s purpose is to work for world peace and improve the conditions of people all over the world.

A major achievement of the U.N. was the Universal Declaration of Human

Eleanor Roosevelt and the Declaration of Human Rights, displayed in Spanish, which was approved by all the United Nations' voting countries

Rights, which was adopted in 1948. Eleanor Roosevelt, the widow of U.S. President Franklin Roosevelt, helped write the declaration. President Roosevelt had led the United States during World War II until his death in 1945. In a speech urging the U.N. to accept the Declaration of Human Rights, Eleanor Roosevelt said, "Man's desire for peace lies behind this declaration. The realization that the flagrant violation of human rights by Nazi and Fascist countries sowed the seeds of the last world war has supplied the impetus for the work, which brings us to the moment of achievement here today." The declaration's preamble noted the role that the Holocaust played in inspiring nations to guarantee the human rights of all people.

Nations have made treaties and agreements to enforce the principles of the Declaration of Human Rights. Acts of genocide still occur. Unlike what happened during the Holocaust, however, international organizations often step in and try to prevent or stop the slaughter of human beings. International laws, and people and organizations that tell the story of the Holocaust and other crimes against humanity, form part of a worldwide effort to stop such tragedies from happening again.

1919
Adolf Hitler joins what becomes the Nazi Party

November 11, 1923
Hitler is arrested after trying to overthrow the German government three days earlier

1929-1933
Nazis gain many votes by promising work and dignity for Aryans and by blaming Jews for Germany's problems

September 29, 1933
The Nazi government forbids Jews to own land

September 15, 1935
The Nazi government strips Jews of German citizenship

1935-1938
The Nazis pass many laws taking away the remaining rights of Jews

1941
Top Nazis work out the details of the Final Solution, and mass killing of Jews begins in Nazi-occupied Europe

Spring 1942
The mass murder of Jews in gas chambers begins at Belzec, Auschwitz-Birkenau, and other camps

Timeline

Hitler becomes Germany's chancellor
January 30, 1933

March 22, 1933
Dachau, the first of many concentration camps, opens

Nazi mobs destroy Jewish businesses and synagogues and kill hundreds of Jews during Kristallnacht
November 9, 1938

1939
Germany invades Czechoslovakia and Poland; World War II begins

Germany is defeated by the Allies; Hitler and Himmler commit suicide; prisoners are freed from concentration camps

1944–1945
Nazis try to hide their crimes by destroying gas chambers and marching prisoners away from death camps

1945

Glossary

anti-Semitism—prejudice or discrimination against Jewish people

armistice—agreement between warring sides to stop fighting

banality—lacking originality; ordinariness

Communist—supporter of an economic system in which property is owned by the government or community and profits are shared; personal freedoms are often limited

concentration camp—prison camp built by Nazis to hold Jews and others, including Communists and anti-Nazi political activists, Jehovah's Witnesses, homosexuals, those they called gypsies, and some criminals

conservative—in politics, wanting to avoid major changes and to keep business and industry in private hands

conspiracy—secret plan by a group

Fascist—person who believes in a form of government that promotes extreme nationalism, repression, and anticommunism and is ruled by a dictator

genocide—systematic extermination of an entire national, racial, religious, or ethnic group

inflation—general increase in prices

left—people with liberal or socialist views

liberal—someone who favors progress and reform and the protection of civil liberties; in politics, liberals are said to be on the left

offensive—organized attack, often during war

persecuted—continually treated in a cruel and unfair way

propaganda—information spread to try to influence the thinking of people; often not completely true or fair

purged—cleaned out by getting rid of unwanted things or unwanted people

resentment—bad feelings from being treated unfairly

right—people with conservative or fascist views

socialist—follower of an economic system in which the government owns most businesses

Third Reich—official name of the Nazi regime that ruled Germany from 1933 to 1945

Additional Resources

Further Reading

Boyne, John. *The Boy in the Striped Pajamas: A Fable*. New York: David Fickling Books, 2006.

Downing, David. *The Nazi Death Camps*. Milwaukee: World Almanac Library, 2006.

Haugen, Brenda. *Adolf Hitler: Dictator of Nazi Germany*. Minneapolis: Compass Point Books, 2006.

Haugen, Brenda. *The Holocaust Museum*. Minneapolis: Compass Point Books, 2008.

Rubin, Susan Goldman. *The Anne Frank Case: Simon Wiesenthal's Search for the Truth*. New York: Holiday House, 2009.

Zullo, Allan, and Mara Bovsun. *Survivors: True Stories of Children in the Holocaust*. New York: Scholastic, 2004.

Internet Sites

Use FactHound to find Internet sites related to this book. All of the sites on FactHound have been researched by our staff.

Here's all you do:
Visit *www.facthound.com*
Type in this code: 9780756543921

Select Bibliography

The Anne Frank Center. Anne Frank. *Diary of a Young Girl*. 20 Aug. 2010. www.annefrank.com/who-is-anne-frank/diary-excerpts/

Brecher, Elinor J. "Survivors of 'Voyage of the Damned' Recall Tragic Trip." 14 Dec. 2009. 20 Aug. 2010. *The Miami Herald*. www.miamiherald.com/2009/12/13/1380682/survivors-of-voyage-of-the-damned.html#ixzz0j8csvZcp

The Elie Wiesel Foundation for Humanity. Elie Wiesel. "Nobel Prize Speech." 20 Aug. 2010. www.eliewieselfoundation.org/nobelprizespeech.aspx

The Hannah Arendt Papers. Jerome Kohn. "Evil: The Crime Against Humanity." 20 Aug. 2010. http://memory.loc.gov/ammem/arendthtml/essayc7.html

The Holocaust History Project. 20 Aug. 2010. www.holocaust-history.org/quote.cgi?source20

Internet Modern History Sourcebook. E.L. Woodward and Rohan Riftlep. *Documents on British Foreign Policy, 1919–1939*. 20 Aug. 2010. www.fordham.edu/halsall/mod/hitler-obersalzberg.html

Jewish Virtual Library. "Goebbels and the "Big Lie."" 20 Aug. 2010. www.jewishvirtuallibrary.org/jsource/Holocaust/goebbelslie.html

National Public Radio. "Eyewitness Reports of Nazi Concentration Camps." 20 Aug. 2010. www.npr.org/templates/story/story.php?storyId=4630493

United States Holocaust Memorial Museum. "Holocaust Personal Histories." 20 Aug. 2010. www.ushmm.org/museum/exhibit/online/phistories/

University of Colorado at Boulder Peace and Conflict Studies. Chris McMorran and Norman Schultz. "Genocide." August 2003. 20 Aug. 2010. http://peacestudies.conflictresearch.org/essay/war_crimes_genocide/

Wood, Angela Gluck. *Holocaust: The Events and Their Impact on Real People*. New York: DK Publishing, 2007.

Yale Law School. "Nuremberg Trial Proceedings Volume 4." 3 Jan. 1946. 20 Aug. 2010. http://avalon.law.yale.edu/imt/01-03-46.asp

Source Notes

Chapter 1: Angela Gluck Wood. *Holocaust: The Events and Their Impact on Real People*. New York: DK Publishing, 2007, p. 40.

Chapter 2: Jewish Virtual Library. "Goebbels and the "Big Lie."" 20 Aug. 2010. www.jewishvirtuallibrary.org/jsource/Holocaust/goebbelslie.html

Chapter 3: Internet Modern History Sourcebook. E.L. Woodward and Rohan Riftlep. *Documents on British Foreign Policy, 1919–1939*. 20 Aug. 2010. www.fordham.edu/halsall/mod/hitler-obersalzberg.html

Chapter 4: The Anne Frank Center. Anne Frank. *Diary of a Young Girl*. 20 Aug. 2010. www.annefrank.com/who-is-anne-frank/diary-excerpts/

Chapter 5: The Holocaust History Project. 20 Aug. 2010. www.holocaust-history.org/quote.cgi?source20

Chapter 6: The Elie Wiesel Foundation for Humanity. Elie Wiesel. "Nobel Prize Speech." 20 Aug. 2010. www.eliewieselfoundation.org/nobelprizespeech.aspx

About the Author

Darlene R. Stille is the award-winning author of more than 80 books for young people, including collections of biographies. She grew up in Chicago and attended the University of Illinois, where she discovered her love of writing. She now lives and writes in Michigan.

Index

Arendt, Hannah, 54–55
Aryans, 4, 18–19, 20, 23, 30

Babi Yar Massacre, 38
Berlin, Germany, 22, 47
boycotts, 4, 29–30

children, 4, 21–22, 24, 38, 41–42, 52
citizenship, 4, 9, 29
Communists, 8, 10–11, 12, 14, 19–20, 25–26, 27, 38
concentration camps, 4, 14, 26, 30–31, 32–34, 36, 39, 49, 52–53 54
conservatives, 8, 12, 13
crematoriums, 39, 46, 48
Czechoslovakia, 4, 25

death camps. *See* extermination camps.
Death's Head Divisions, 35
diseases, 33–34, 49, 50

economy, 4, 7–8, 9, 18
education, 4, 14, 17–18, 20, 22
Eichmann, Adolf, 36, 54, 55
Eichmann in Jerusalem: A Report on the Banality of Evil (Hannah Arendt), 54
elections, 7, 12–13, 14
employment, 7, 9, 11, 18, 20
Enabling Act, 14
extermination camps, 4, 34, 36, 39–41, 41–42, 42–46, 48

Fascists, 8, 9, 56
Final Solution, 4, 35
food, 4, 26, 33, 40, 49
France, 4, 6, 25, 26, 47
Frank, Anne, 29

Garfinkel, Paula, 33
gas chambers, 4, 38–39, 41–42, 42–46, 48
gas vans, 38
German army, 6, 8, 10, 12, 17–18, 25, 33, 38
Germany, 4, 5–6, 7–8, 9, 11–12, 12–13, 14–15, 16, 17–18, 19, 20, 22, 23, 24–26, 27, 28, 29, 30, 31, 32–33, 47, 49, 52

Gestapo (secret police), 28, 29, 30–31, 35–36
ghettos, 31–32, 33, 36, 40
Goebbels, Joseph, 17, 20, 52
Great Britain, 4, 25, 26, 27
Gruber, Ruth, 6

Hannah Arendt Center, 55
Heydrich, Reinhard, 35–36
Himmler, Heinrich, 35–36, 52
Hindenburg, Paul von, 12–13, 14, 16
Hitler, Adolf, 4, 5, 9–12, 13–14, 16, 17, 18, 19, 20, 23, 24, 25, 27, 28, 29, 52
Hitler Youth, 21–22, 23

invasions, 4, 23, 24–25, 25–26, 26–27, 28, 31, 35, 38, 47
Italy, 4, 9, 27
Itzkowitz, Sam, 44–46

Japan, 4, 27

Kiev, Ukraine, 38
Kohn, Jerome, 55
Kristallnacht, 30

labor camps, 4, 33, 40, 42, 44
laws, 13, 14, 23, 29, 30, 57
League of German Girls, 21
liberation, 49–50
living space, 24, 25
Lynch, Pat, 51

marriage, 29
mass graves, 46
medical experiments, 33–34, 42
Mein Kampf (Adolf Hitler), 9, 19
mobile killing units, 36–39
Mogilensky, Emma, 22
Mussolini, Benito, 9

nationalists, 8–9
National Ministry of Public Enlightenment and Propaganda, 20
newspapers, 14, 20, 29
Nuremberg, Germany, 22, 29, 52–53

Ohlendorf, Otto, 36–38

Poland, 4, 25, 26–27, 31–32, 33, 39, 40, 42, 44–45, 48
police, 4, 14, 16, 28, 30, 38, 40, 52
propaganda, 10, 17, 18–20, 23, 52
property, 4, 30

rallies, 10–11, 22–23
Reichstag building, 14
Roosevelt, Eleanor, 56–57
Roosevelt, Franklin, 56
Rose, James A., 49

Schneiderman, Leo, 42
Schutzstaffel (SS), 16, 30–31, 35, 36, 38, 40, 41, 42, 43, 44, 45, 46, 49
slave labor, 32, 33, 39, 40, 42, 44–45
Social Democratic Party, 19
Soviet Union, 4, 26–27, 35, 36, 38, 46, 47
speeches, 10, 19, 20, 23, 56–57
Star of David, 4
Sturmabteilung (SA), 10–11, 15
Sudetenland, 25
swastikas, 6, 22

transportation, 6, 29, 36, 37–38, 40, 41
Treaty of Versailles, 6, 10, 11, 12, 25

United Nations, 55–56
United States, 4, 6, 26, 27, 50–51, 52, 56
Universal Declaration of Human Rights, 55–57

war crimes trials, 36–37, 52–53, 54–55
Weimar Republic, 7–8, 9, 10, 12
Wiesel, Elie, 47
World War I, 5–6, 10, 12, 17–18, 25
World War II, 4, 21, 23, 24, 26–28, 36, 55, 56